The Copy Cat

Paul Shipton

Illustrated by

David Mostyn

OXFORD
UNIVERSITY PRESS

Nick saw a cat and picked it up.
"Put that down!" said Kaz. "It's
a Copy Cat!"

The Copy Cat jumped out of
Nick's hands and hit his Bug.
The Bug fell and smashed,
and the cat ran into
the school.

The Copy Cat hid and looked at the children. When the children had gone, the cat ran out.

Nick and Kaz looked and
looked for the cat.
"You check the classroom,"
said Kaz. "I'll get some water."

Nick didn't see the cat in the classroom. There was just one person there.

"Hello, Tizz," said Nick.

Nick went out and waited for Kaz.
Just then Tizz walked past.
"Oh!" said Nick. "But I saw you in
the classroom just now!"

Nick told Tizz about the Copy Cat.
"You didn't see me," said Tizz.
"You saw a *copy* of me. That's
what Copy Cats do!"

The Copy Cat Tizz was at the window. There were lots of Copy Cats at the back of the school. The Copy Cat Tizz let them all in.

The new Copy Cats looked at
the Copy Cat Tizz and then...
They made more Tizzes!

When Nick and the *real* Tizz got there, the classroom was full of Copy Cat Tizzes. Lots and lots of Copy Cat Tizzes...

A Copy Cat Tizz pulled in
the real Tizz.

"Oh no!" said Nick. "Where is
the *real* one now?"

Nick held out his Bug.

"The real Tizz can fix things,"
he said. "So who can fix this?"
But *all* the Tizzes ran for the Bug.
"I can!" they all said.

"I've got the water!" said Kaz.
The Tizzes looked afraid. Just one
Tizz jumped in front of Nick's Bug.
"No!" he said. "Water is bad
for Bugs!"

"*This* is the real Tizz!" said Nick.
He pulled Tizz away and Kaz
threw the water at the Copy Cat
Tizzes. They ran for the window.

"They all ran away from the water," said Nick with a grin. "Yes," said Kaz. "That's what Copy Cats do!"